DOG STAR

BY THE SAME AUTHOR

POETRY

Soft Keys
Raising Sparks
Burning Babylon
Corpus
The Half Healed
Drysalter
Selected Poems
Mancunia
Ransom

FICTION

Patrick's Alphabet
Breath

NON-FICTION

Edgelands (with Paul Farley)
Deaths of the Poets (with Paul Farley)
Quartet for the End of Time

DOG STAR

Michael Symmons Roberts

CAPE POETRY

1 3 5 7 9 10 8 6 4 2

Jonathan Cape, an imprint of Vintage, is part of the Penguin Random House group of companies

Vintage, Penguin Random House UK, One Embassy Gardens,
8 Viaduct Gardens, London SW11 7BW

penguin.co.uk/vintage
global.penguinrandomhouse.com

First published by Jonathan Cape in 2026

Copyright © Michael Symmons Roberts 2026

The moral right of the author has been asserted

Penguin Random House values and supports copyright. Copyright fuels creativity, encourages diverse voices, promotes freedom of expression and supports a vibrant culture. Thank you for purchasing an authorised edition of this book and for respecting intellectual property laws by not reproducing, scanning or distributing any part of it by any means without permission. You are supporting authors and enabling Penguin Random House to continue to publish books for everyone. No part of this book may be used or reproduced in any manner for the purpose of training artificial intelligence technologies or systems. In accordance with Article 4(3) of the DSM Directive 2019/790, Penguin Random House expressly reserves this work from the text and data mining exception.

Typeset in 11/13pt Bembo Book MT Pro by Six Red Marbles UK, Thetford, Norfolk
Printed and bound in Great Britain by TJ Books, Padstow, Cornwall

The authorised representative in the EEA is Penguin Random House Ireland,
Morrison Chambers, 32 Nassau Street, Dublin D02 YH68

A CIP catalogue record for this book is available from the British Library

ISBN 9781787336032

Penguin Random House is committed to a sustainable future
for our business, our readers and our planet. This book is made
from Forest Stewardship Council® certified paper.

for Ellis

CONTENTS

I

Sumac	3
Salitter	4
Night Fox	5
Snow-Remembering Heart	6
Wunderkammer	8
Mandelstam Variables – I	9
Two Women Walk a Himalayan Wolf	10
Metaphysical Animals	12
Greys	14
You are Dust	16
Mandelstam Variables – II	17

II

Their Deaths	21
Eurasian Blackbird	22
Grey Seal	24
Mandelstam Variables – III	25
Ramson Flies	26
Spruce Cone	27
British Summer Time	28
Maquette for a Wildfire	30
Mandelstam Variables – IV	32
Kiss on Wood	33
Astrov's Maps	34
Mandelstam Variables – V	35

III

Orchestrion	39
Taxonomy	40
Gentian Liqueur	42
Mandelstam Variables – VI	43
Eight Lab Mice	44
Pied Wagtails	47
Mandelstam Variables – VII	48
Aquarium	49
Free Dive	54
On Grace	55

IV

Mandelstam Variables – VIII	59
Hound	60
Elliptics	62
A Winter Inventory	65
Red Smoky Hearts	66
Soliloquy of a Focus-Puller	67
Notes & Acknowledgements	69

I

'If even a dog's tooth is truly worshipped, it glows with light'
Iris Murdoch

SUMAC

In a back street between warehouses,
fly-tipped tyres and oil drums, walls
falling into the square they denote,
this single relic of a long-gone garden:
staghorn trunk and boughs, part-beast, part-plant,
low enough to climb in. Too perfect to fell.
A car idles in the next yard.
Crow on a rooftop picks at its breast.

A woman climbs down from the sumac,
brushing herself off, hunched and crooked,
clothes covered in moss, worn thin.
She has been up there since childhood,
when this was still a garden.
Someone is calling her back to the house,
because everyone is waiting at the table.
Up beyond, the loud wild rises.

SALITTER

Last snow salts the tails
of bullfinches blushed pink with cold.
On every roof alike it lands
with tenderness as if to dress a wound.
In our blanked-out road, a patch of rock salt
with a cast of rust opens like a rose.
Under dead skies, a heart grows in this thaw,
too hot to hold, cut and bruised,
a shaking, naked heart too bulbous for a bird's,
too modest to keep a horse in blood.
It must be yours, this gift, left outside
your house, listen, this is hope, the meat of it,
salitter, essence of life, of love,
ungovernable electricity, the stuff of us,
not drying out but thawing. Take it.
For an instant, the astonishment
cuts through, then melts away.

NIGHT FOX

Stripped of its man-suit,
one young dog fox halts,
mid-step, halfway across the lawn.
It's four-o-nine, so no-one sees this,
but the next day, in another city,
I scroll through last night's footage
on my phone in a ritual performance
of control, halted at a crossing,
waiting for the lights to change,
lined up streetside in a row
of suits and trainers, coffee-carriers,
backpacks, when I catch his eye.

He must have snagged on
the doorbell camera's motion light,
not just a thought, this fox,
no messenger or symbol,
but the real presence, disassembled
and reconstituted out of digits.
Flesh he was for all that, fleeting too
like me, though when I met his eye
he was already long-gone,
underground or on the take
or laid in bas-relief beside a road.
We have come a long way both.

SNOW-REMEMBERING HEART

Eighth of March,
the standoff breaks,
weeks of winter-spring

on shuffle.
Now it only goes one way.
Thrushes in the ash

can hear the roar
of mass mitoses –
sheer, rude force of life,

nothing hesitant
or tender in this
mighty rush of love:

un-stemmable,
unstable, volatile, holy,
a wild, wild voltage.

Blackthorn,
first out from death,
while other trees stay

stick and bone,
this frozen blast,
all stake and nails,

blossom as moth swarm,
each five-petalled flower
its own explosion:

dense white dwarf stars
drawn too close,
caught the tail of winter

turned to ice on impact,
now an arch of them,
a starlit colonnade

for us to pass through
on our way to spring.
Stand and count the lamps.

WUNDERKAMMER

Were it not for their pins, these specimens
– bluebottles, beetle-gems, puffed-up bees –
would flitter in their shallow,
glass-topped drawer,
or so goes the illusion,

like the mutter of an old projector
running one last film, its final frame a dragonfly,
more solid than the rest,
its shoulder stripes' pale ochre,
its welded ten-piece chassis,
posed as latent flight
in that split-second before taking off,
only to be let down by its wings.
Who cares? Let them shiver into dust.

Outside, mayflies on strings bob
on parked cars' roofs, a mile from any river,
but they shine – all sex and fury –
mouthless icons of brevity, these dayflies,
driven by an overwhelming purpose,
fierce in their eternity.

MANDELSTAM VARIABLES – I

Where are you and what are the chances
of a visitation, to lift this godforsaken
brutish day: a gold blow-in clump,
a gust-cut cloud of seed clocks
caught in the crab apple's fingertips?

Rarely seen alone, goldfinch wonder-clusters
glow at midnight in the city's perma-light.
What's the weather like in your eyes?

Behind your forehead you hold no
wheel of colours, but millennia of harmonics,
a hard-won hard-wired catalogue
of tunes so tough to sing that you
would sooner parrot songs of any neighbour.

Come back to us, we miss you!
Your blood-dipped face, inverse pearl eyes.
I'll wait the night and watch, petition you,

and look, the sourpuss tree in April
has held back its tulle and tissue pinks,
which while it augurs badly means
a chance for me to pick you out –
rare baubles in the branch-top jackstraws.

But these words contain their own negation.
For every goldfinch put into a poem,
one will vanish from the world outside.

TWO WOMEN WALK A HIMALAYAN WOLF

Because it has outgrown its rosewood cage;
so while a new one – twice the size and more ornate -
is being made beneath the empress trees,
they lead it on a rope, to unknot its mighty haunches,
stretch its balled-up sinews.

When it wins their trust they want to give it
the run of their house, but now
they walk it through the boulevards, or it walks them,
past a gallery full of screens, a hall of mirrors, freak shows,
a museum of the creatures,
stuffed and posed in tall glass cases.

Shopkeepers, masseurs, thieves bow their heads
to the majesty of this tame beast as it lopes,
nose up, locked onto the vanishing point ahead.
Two women's long brocaded coats,
are sparking, charged from the rub against its fur.
They know full well the scent it's caught is forest-deep
– leaves, rot, seeds, nuts –
with sharper notes of mountain air beyond.

Natural selection has built this wolf to flourish
at high altitudes, its huge lungs thrive
in thinnest air, so there will come a point
when they must drop the leash and watch their pet
climb out of their lives. But not yet.
Two women adore their Himalayan Wolf
for its agouti coat, the pepper on its muzzle,
the way it sings itself to sleep.

Is it instinct or memory that guides them?
The slack rope tightens and their coats sweep back.
Two women run behind a Himalayan Wolf.
Ahead of them, a thickening sky, a presence,
a growing awareness that despite their love,
nothing here will slake its raging thirst for heights.

METAPHYSICAL ANIMALS

At first light,
night workers
fumble on doorsteps for their house-keys,
let themselves back in,
already half asleep.

Twin magpies comb the lawn in lockstep.
Magnolia in the park has gone full candelabra
weeks too soon,
petals tobacco-tipped.

A trader in futures joins the silent choir
waiting for the day's first train.

A scrub bush with no genus,
self-seeded, unseen,
scales the back wall
of a house that will change hands this year,
in need of renovation.

They have left the back door open.
Now a redbreast drops in,
stunned by the hallway's sudden dark,
the cold stone floor.

Its bold heart brings fire into the house,
where a daughter washes her mother
– unthinkable a year ago –
by candlelight,
music on the radio,
skin blemished, watercoloured, foxed.

This is both grace and favour.
Everything hurts.
Nothing will.

GREYS

This cut was laid for trains,
tracks torn up, sold for scrap a lifetime back,
the old line now a road to nowhere.

No trace of the neat, branch halt,
just a gritstone slab of platform under thorns.
Three squirrels set like squat traps

snap and jump, three tree-rats, nimble, limber
ash-tree acrobats run branches to their tips
then leap to a neighbour in the copse,

spirits of smoke, these young ones,
tails more notional than real,
more smoke than fur, more cloud than smoke,

to match these morning skies.
It's May, still cold, too soon to hope –
kite-winds, hard rains incoming.

Do they want our attention, or our absence,
these three spindles, jittery
hair-triggered shadow-tails, do they?

An intermittent charge bolts through them.
Every branch they touch, emboldened now,
braves a show of snow flowers.

Hoarders, full of flaunt, dart and feint,
fainter-hearted than their tails will tell,
ghosts of creatures like those families lined up

on the platform at this dead-end stop,
posing in their winter clothes,
mouths full of dust,

straight-backed for the camera on the day
they left the mills for good, went west,
a one-off print long lost between the pages

of a travellers' guide, émigrés in *eigengrau*,
faces pale to salt, their then futures
now part of the voracious past.

YOU ARE DUST

A city stuck in winter,
faux sun outside a faux-tropical bar,
menu board of technicolour drinks,
mixologist in a beach shirt,
murals of parrots.

Tight for time, I half-run for my train,
pass the plastic palms,
and ash falls on my tongue.
It all comes back:
the annual enactment,
a mock-triumphal entry,
palm frond fletches waved as fans,
leaf crosses our boys used as swords,
boxed for a year then burnt.

It is not guilt, to miss the silent queue,
the thumbprint cross,
the muttered line that tells me what I am,
– a brief coalescence of matter –
Not guilt, but lack.
A naked brow, unbruised, no mark,
no jolt in mirrors and shop windows,
no itch that makes me leave it,
until I forget and brush it off.

Train on time for once,
standing room only.
Next to me, a child with a cat box,
and inside, no cat but a bearded dragon.
Its arrowhead face nods and nods,
in answer to some
long-forgotten impulse.

MANDELSTAM VARIABLES – II

Hello? You in the headphones,
did you learn your trade from bats?
Or even better, wax moths
who out-shrill the shrillest bat?
Or dolphins? Or dogs?
Do you get benchmarked for
surveillance skills? Double-pay
when you graduate from owl to rat?
These exile nights will never leave me:
wired in to a half-tuned radio,
waiting for the time signal
at the top of each hour.
Has Spring come where you are?
Buds letting go their winter clench?
I can out-listen you.
However hard you strain at me,
I hold you in the silence,
between my finger and my thumb,
and I can hear you squirm.

II

'The scent of these armpits is aroma finer than prayer'
                                               Walt Whitman

THEIR DEATHS

They were impossible, like rumoured orchids:
all quake on a cold peak too remote to contemplate.

Each summer's rise and fall just hammered home
the unreality of their deaths, so in the absence

of serious evidence their deaths became a myth,
which only made it stranger when they came.

Their deaths dropped on their shoulders like old coats,
threadbare from years of shrugging on to venture out.

There was no mountain, bloom, no distance ever.
No-one let their deaths steal in through open windows.

Truth is, their deaths had been here all along.
But you know all of this. All of us know but don't.

Drain the pipes of water, shut off the power.
Now bag those clothes. Someone could use them.

EURASIAN BLACKBIRD

You dark of plumage,
darker still of voice,
denizen of deepest wildwoods,

you who drew yourself
through countless generations
into gardens and suburban parks

primeval singer with a modern
repertoire, you showy,
you sassy, you spindrift,

you priest who starts an evensong
across this continent
in spring, you sunbather

on dry-baked lawns,
splayed like a broken paper fan,
cat's crime scene,

you whose eye I must not
catch for fear of being pulled in
through the halo

then your honeycomb iris
into the negative space
where a pupil should be,

where you hold the old woods,
dense and slow with song:
all beasts, shadows, shafts of sun

distilled into a ripe full-stop.
If you scare now while I'm in there
I will never leave.

GREY SEAL

It is the stink of you,
the thousand-fetid-oceans' concentrate,
the gag, that I can call up still,

seal as washed-up pelt-balloon
burst by rocks chucked
from the cliff-edge path,

so two weeks on you were
a fly-blown open wound that drew
the dog to climb inside,

to writhe and roll until
alive with you, a fish-gut stench
that made us retch, but still a perfume

rare and rarefied as incense,
rank and high, life on life, flesh on flesh,
a rude, loud rot,

this proof of life in death,
more glorious than scentless stars,
or snowflakes' cold geometry,

this easter fire our dog dragged in,
your reek her second skin
that never quite wore off.

MANDELSTAM VARIABLES – III

Overrated earth, this.
Over-tilled and over-dug,
pumped up, primped
like a dolled-up cadaver,
clapped out, shabby,
like a warhorse gone to seed.
This dark earth would sooner
close over your coffin lid
than break your fall
or honour you with garlands.
When lovers walk on it,
this earth will serenade them
with rain-sodden flutes,
asthmatic clarinets.
The land is not what it's
cracked up to be. Plough it.
Fold it into itself for good.
Give up hope of living here,
it's spent. Head to the coast,
learn to fish, comb a beach,
build castles there,
at least on sand their ruin
comes as quickly as the tide,
not built to last. Swim
until it's out of sight.
Good luck, dark earth!
Stay wide-eyed, bold.
See what, in our absence,
can be conjured from
your rich, dark reticence.

RAMSON FLIES

This woodland hums.
My boots release wild garlic plumes
and with them, you —
squab-headed, gun-grey striped, antennae
lit like firebrands in the evening shade.

I could cup you in my hands,
release you three trees down the path
into another world,
your universe pulled inside out,
but love will not allow it
— call it love, or fear
that fate might do the same to me.

A postcard on my wall has ancient lovers
greet a rooster's dawn song
with a burning arrow to prolong their night.
This painted scene is framed by
a rectangle of nascent buds on midnight blue,
another frame of floral hearts,
within a frame of ivy twine.

And as their night of love is held,
defended by those frames,
so your close world
is held in place by frames of soil, leaf,
glade, cloud, each life spent
on and in a single bulb of allium.

SPRUCE CONE

I can't recall the details now,
just that I found it far, far north:
a frosted forest floor and it
inflamed by midnight sun,
a millefeuille trap,

touched by time outside time,
turned into a treasure,
pocketed as if it held some trace
of fugitive, unstable daylight.

Once or twice a year
I pick it up, offer every angle
to the window's gaze.
It is a perfect paper model of itself,

one cold summer's abstruse intricacy,
pangolin-scaled, pliable,
I strum it like a thumb piano,
lift each chevron, blow out
what it keeps of us in dust.

BRITISH SUMMER TIME

Old smokers on the rec
are first to perceive that the light
has less bite to it,

or their dogs do as they loop
and churn the football pitch
in endless,

circular pursuit. There is some
currency, fizz of a charge
for the first time

since last year's leaves let fall.
New ones, frog tongues,
green the branch tips.

Who are the fools now?
A yellow car slides past the gate
and sudden sun

sets it off like a flashgun.
Each year I wonder what this
lost hour would have held,

but it came in the night
and I slept through it, missed
the jump cut,

glitch in cat wails, owl calls,
in the field behind our house,
the earth's rough splice

makes water judder
in the pipes, crockery rattles
in the cupboards.

MAQUETTE FOR A WILDFIRE

Off the beaten track – to put some
earth between me and the cross-moor road –

weeks back I found a sympathetic cure:
a snag of sheep's wool on a hand

of dried-up heather, its fake smoke so real
I coughed as if it caught my throat.

I took it as a talisman, mocked-up to fool the fire
its work had just begun,

to give this land some time to mend.
So this is why it hasn't come, the final burn.

I could never find that place again,
the wool no doubt long gone, shrugged off,

heather back in purple, but still
on steaming nights, awake in the next town,

I pray for reassurance that this blaze in wool
will keep us safe until first light.

Heatwaves north of here are blackening the hills.
Stonechat, skylark, snipe

all flown, their half-formed ground nests
– never more than keel prints

in the moor grass, barely an impression –
now gone up like paper-twists.

Only the mountain hare has guile and sorcery
to stand tall like a heron in a river,

then to dance between the flames
when they arrive. Now we are next in line:

these peaks a spark away from wasteland,
one dog-end with a tail of smoke will do it.

MANDELSTAM VARIABLES – IV

> Mute as unprinted paper,
> this apartment. Bare walls.
> Nothing personal.
> Any fools could live here.
> Only the radiators' indigestion
> breaks our vow of silence,
> though we can't recall
> the reason why we made it.
> All is immaculate. Calm.
> All except the telephone,
> a squat frog ever primed to leap.
> Our few possessions hate the place.
> They long to leave. And me?
> I play tunes for invisible ears,
> teach goldfinch riffs to killers.
> My reading is ration books.
> My listening is speeches by the dead.
> My songs are screams dressed as salves.
> I am an artist. I work from life.
> I am a moth caught in a fist.
> I am the salt left in a pan.

KISS ON WOOD

Horse underwater,
driven off the seawall
for some ritual or revenge,
ran until its legs
were taken by the weeds,
tail and mane as currents —
handsome head a slipstream,
torso towed behind -
until this chase through sea
became inseparable
from what the ocean was.
Lungs gave in.
Whole histories rose and fell.
Seas shrank back to land.
Today I chanced upon
— in marram grass, on dunes —
a driftwood horse,
petrified at full speed,
otherworldly as a comet tail,
its own creation myth.
Now my chapped lips
smart with salt.

ASTROV'S MAPS

Late summer, later than we thought,
Sirius becomes a second sun,
two stars rising and setting in sync,

too much power, too much heat to bear.
Streets empty, food rots on shelves,
refrigerators burn out trying to keep a hold on it.

All of us catch fever, so the only way to pass days
is to lie motionless in blacked-out rooms,
listening to flies trapped in the walls.

At night, the doctor sits beneath a lamp,
paints maps from last year's inventories:
trees by hectare, bears by tracks, hawks by kills.

Every year he makes a new map:
green tapered back, lakes shrunk to pools,
rivers into slate tracks over what we still call farms.

Once the dog days pass, he goes house to house
to register the dead, to see who made it through,
unrolls his maps on our tables to show us

how woods are failing, tightening to coppice,
thicket, down to a single talismanic oak,
as if his painstaking cartography

– admittedly a glory in itself –
amounts to any kind of agency.
As soon as he leaves we lower the blinds.

MANDELSTAM VARIABLES – V

Maybe madness starts like this.
Remote. No threat.
A thousand miles from you
in some ruined cathedral
where a spider is caught
by a javelin of light
through what was once a window.
Or maybe this is sanity.
That shaft of sunlight scans
across a continent to touch you.
Now your house fills up with guests,
instant friends with no wants
but your company, a feast of love,
and everyone is undefended.
This happens here on earth
as music swells from room to room,
not in some floating paradise.
What a vision – even to imagine it!
No. Wait. What am I saying?
Apologies are due.
Do, please, forgive me.
Now (whisper) under your breath,
please read it back to me.

III

I'll tell you how the Sun rose – / A Ribbon at a time
                                          Emily Dickinson

ORCHESTRION

Dry grasses, beech leaves'
parchment paper.
Among this spent
pale splendour
one stripped wing,
an ocean-crosser once,
now picked clean.
A row of bleached,
bare quills mounted on
a hand-crank bone,
its body carried off
in some soft mouth.
A comb that holds a tune
but lacks a box
to sound it out.
Come on, you souls,
put a current through
this remnant –
the crackle, arc of grace,
full voltage of life.
Play us what it says.

TAXONOMY

The night you died I was counting,
on the drive to you, how many houses
still had lights on in the small hours,
adding up the digits on their gates and doors.

Then ceiling-tiles above your deathbed
(we knew it was that as soon as we saw it)
from door to window, wall to wall,
to calculate the total in the room,

but none of this contained my grief.
So since that night, I broke the world down
into categories, sub-sets, all the trees
no longer simply trees,

but broadleaves, needles, those that weep.
Birdsong sorted into falsetto trills,
then coos, then caws, then twist again
and map the riffs, the skittish loops.

I kept a list of fallen leaves,
of the hours I slept at night.
I kept a note of times the first and last cars
of each day took the hill towards the pass.

I spent a year in the seed merchants
where your grandad worked,
and counted every seed that came in,
every seed that went out in a paper bag.

The staff and customers were dead
a century ago, the seed shop now a bar.
It was not that counting helped at all,
just that it mattered.

I set out in a coal-boat on the Irish Sea
which went down in a storm and took your
great grandfather with it,
and I counted all the cod, hake, pollack,

sand eels, dogfish, skate, all the uncaught.
When all relevant lists were made
I called it quits. The trouble with these counts
was that as soon as one was done,

its reckonings were overrun,
so now I count my squandered, restless days,
and print each new one bold
before I lose the look of it.

GENTIAN LIQUEUR

Translucent with a taint of rheum,
gift from a friend in Germany,
my father took it as a joke,
offered round at Christmas, or to visitors,
while he stuck to his scotch.

A shot glass of this hard, clear draught,
then watch their faces as its
distillate of dark, of alpine nights,
slipped down like bitter honey,
then the coughing.

A decade since he fell into the past,
their house now cleared
to make way for the living,
this half-gone bottle stands
at the back of our fridge –
lid sealed shut, untouched, undrinkable.

What is it holding there,
some ante-light before the full light comes?
A blue so dark it reads as clear,
counterweight to the furnace
we saw through the curtain.

MANDELSTAM VARIABLES – VI

Wildcat city. Crouched. Coiled.
Light on a patrol car beats like a blue heart.
On the outskirts, an empty bread van
speeds home to meet the curfew.
A cuckoo, mad as befits this city,
tells the same joke on repeat
in a belltower without a bell,
– ropes cut, change-ringers dead –
but I, for one night only,
walk as I choose, unwatched, ungrounded,
along the rim of the abyss.
One day, you and I will meet.
I've been rehearsing for it,
a speech that will unlock it all for us,
though I fear words will fail us again.
Perhaps we'll fill our mouths with bread,
so much that talking is impossible.
Just laugh at our gluttony.
The wildcat will doze at our feet.

EIGHT LAB MICE

On the night of 25th May 1940, at Oxford's Dunn School of Pathology, the efficacy of penicillin was proven in eight mice with streptococcus – half given the treatment, half not.

i

Now is when we wake up, all whole of us,
all lives held close in this one room
footsteps on floors above, a scent of love,
world of us you cannot enter

seemingly well, asleep but well
one staggering four steps then fell
others seemingly perfectly well

ii

distant pasts, a roil of, fusillade of, cascade
of us, unfolding ever, us upon us upon,
young upon young, daylight climbs,
a box of it, a cuboid, trap-like, falls

one barely alive
twitched once or twice
I draw a crimson cross

iii

must of us, a muskiness, mus musculus,
well-fed, well-met, laid on a bed of wheat husks
subcutaneous, needling, necromancy,
streptococcus streptococci

three mice left in group one
each new breath they look more drunk
one sick with laboured breath

iv

dusk draws down, our room turns subfusc

one lifted its head and gasped for breath
I draw a crimson cross
three and four respiration slower now

v

sirens outside, silence inside, save the so-high
only we can hear, indifferent to fear so no
need for an elegy, as we see all of us

one staggered a short distance at nine
it looks half-dead
I draw a crimson cross

vi

four walls of steel and air, across the world
out there, our watched, recorded cage

one alive from control group
fourth mouse very sick at ten
group two all fair, one eye discharge

vii

stand-in for a bigger beast, stunt-double, dupe,
microscopic life studies, we glorious nobodies

fourth mouse now dead,
I draw a crimson cross
surviving four look fit and well

viii

a heart's extent is breached, a beachhead won,
whenever there is sun or bulb our black eyes
each will hold a single distant star,
together we bear constellations

survivors look in perfect health
all four alive after two weeks
growing nimbler, stronger by the day

PIED WAGTAILS

What is this work you do?
Tonight, on my walk
back from the overworld,
I hear a river undercut my road,
stop on the bridge, lean over,
there you are, dab-dip and flicker,
cast in streetlights' amber,
soft traps sprung and reset
over and over,
beaks down untying river knots,
needles between stones.
Are you preparing a wind tunnel
under our feet, to funnel gales
from peak to plain,
or will it be a holding place,
not one state or another,
for couples who never
say each other's names aloud.

MANDELSTAM VARIABLES – VII

Drunk on fumes of kerosene,
you and I sit by the stove
through hours of darkness,
one fat loaf our daily bread,
listening to our goldfinch in his cage.
So many of them caught and made
to work as jukeboxes
that out there in the forests
there are too few left
to teach their songs to younger birds,
apostolic succession cut.
In the hour before dawn,
we tie our paper suitcases with string,
leave to catch the first train
to somewhere no cartographer
could ever picture
and no shadow will follow.

AQUARIUM

A human figure held in water
slowed to within an inch of your life,
absolutely caught in it,

or maybe by it, but that's immaterial,
either way it's constant, attendant
at your making and at your undoing,

at the first bath that sent you all howl,
when strong arms lowered you,
a tepid dip not what you needed then,

you as arched plucked bird,
skinned fish, it held you then and still,
or it's falling and you honour the fall,

halt your sprint for shelter,
stand in a rinsed-out city square
head back, fighting to keep your eyes open,

waiters and cooks from the cafés
step out to watch the deluge too,
beckoning you from under awnings,

taxis swerve to miss you,
you as statue, head back to let it gather you,
you alone in the heart of your city,

just you and an old bronze king on a horse,
who is melting on the cobbles
in spite of his pomp, and if you

had clothes on now their colours
would be running, or not a fall but
a weight of it, the sea, a sea, or back up

the throat of an estuary, a choked spring
waits for you to break the dam,
to prise away what stems it,

lie down on its stony bed to cool off,
let it swarm over you, or just your hands
turn in it, over and over until stunned by cold,

or times you thought you did the holding,
a pin-head-studded tumbler of it
left by your bed but untouched,

stubbed when you reached in the night,
shattered and woke the whole hotel
where you take a box-room each winter

pay the rent by washing pots while you
draw up a ledger of lost chances,
your near misses, earn scraps from the kitchen

in exchange for personalised verses of love,
or a drop from blank blue skies on
the rick of your neck in a summer drought,

electric shock of it, threatening monsoon
or a midday heart attack,
but comes to nothing but the drop,

or the bay in a storm on New Year's Eve,
gales too stiff to stand against,
and a couple shouting from a lit boat

too far out, or the thirst for rivers,
the walking miles to find the source, not sure
if you trust it when you do, the overwhelm,

floating cars, house roofs as refuge,
each room an aquarium, horrible
unwitting beauty of the mirrored sun on it

even as it bears away, ungovernable,
frontierless, ground-seeker, spirit-leveller,
giver of everything up to an ocean,

to any sea it meets, diviner of the flaws
in hulls, hairlines, bringer of angler-fish,
sea-snails to rusted containers

stacked with undelivered gifts,
or the times you turned it down for something
stronger, the fact that it's the most of

what you're made of, that and carbon,
a pencil and a drink is you, head down in
a sink so many miles from

home, slow-hearted, how you long
to hold it there, and hold
and hold until your face dissolves,

or the salt bite of it, the boil of it,
how you, in it, lose all the weight you
couldn't shift, or falling overboard, the gasp,

a startle-reflex, trying not to thrash,
willing to believe that effortful stilled limbs
will save you if you don't give in,

or the lift of it, what you take from it unthinking,
the rush of calm when all is fury,
respite with no prospect of a cure,

or outside the infirmary, patients on drips
wheeled out to take the air,
or in the visiting hours

the sips you take from a baby's beaker
held by your daughter or your son
as you did for them,

now you are too frail to lift it,
and all you can say is how fine it is,
how cold and rare and in that moment

how it brings you back to your attention,
or the sluice-down hose on the slab
where you were laid out

in search of causes, reasons,
though by then you were far gone, far out
to sea yourself, heartless now

but more loved than ever and still loving,
or the wade-in, not through,
the fear of what might be in it,

a good fearing, a chest-high walk in it,
or what might rise up in the current,
brush against your back,

the lack of clarity, its limpid gift to us
rendered lethal by this murk,
this ever-teeming other state,

or you stepping out of your grave-pit
coughing up roots, longing for nothing more
than to stride out through a downpour,

or you trying to join the dots,
reading words off floating crates and tins
to find a line you could live by.

FREE DIVE

After dark is best,
since that is when it opens.
Torch beams fingering the cracks
and fissures,
gloves lifting coral, parting weeds.
The length of a breath is all,
the slower the dive,
the longer it will last.
The less I panic the safer it gets,
but blood still rises.

Truth is, it's not
about lobsters or clams,
though I bag them if I find them.
What I'm trying to rediscover is the byss,
not the abyss, but groundless ground,
an absence so utter
I knew I had met God.
A glimpse, once, for a second,
then my breath ran out,
forced me to surface.

My children grew and left.
Bones creak, pulse falters.
But still I look for it,
between a green rock and an umber,
under urchins, brittle stars,
where sea-floor turns mollusk-silk,
fine but fathomless.
The longer this goes on
the more I doubt
it ever happened.

ON GRACE

Against the laws of physics
she has picked herself up
in a hessian sack,
to take the load off her legs,

she has carried herself
to all her old haunts,
her sack-self like a bone-bag cat
warms her feet under the table.

Everyone asks after her.
The florist gives her bulbs,
the baker, crumbs. TVs
she sees through other people's

windows screen familiar scenes,
people long-gone whose lives
must be written down somewhere.
A child she meets halfway

across the painted iron
canal bridge hands her an off-white
cabbage rose as intricate
as her wedding dress.

Jackdaws in the plane trees,
mummers, acting out everyday
scenes from the other side.

IV

'Grace fills empty spaces, but it can only enter where there is a void to receive it, and it is grace itself which makes this void.'
Simone Weil

MANDELSTAM VARIABLES - VIII

Night. Late.
I wash my boots in the yard
under a scatterplot of stars
too pale to catch on my watch-face.
I look up to trace the Dog Star,
the only one I know.
It's always true to me.
No sign of it tonight.
My own cur shivers at the door,
his coat matted with mud and leaf mulch.
I'm locked out,
my keys dropped back along the path.
No chance of finding them.
I've walked an unplanned route for miles,
my head up in the trees
triangulating futures,
running through the sums.
Besides, there's snow.
Aching to fall all day, it settles now.
For the first time in my life,
I feel worlds turn beneath my feet.

HOUND

First night of November,
and there he is again

outside the glass back-door.
All four months of your being,

you have gone to meet him
after sunset, face-to-face,

you in the bright, warm kitchen,
him in a lightless realm of ice,

heads tilted at each other,
whining to be let out or in.

The instant you step over, he is gone,
fugitive too long to cross the line.

Now you stand where he was,
alone out on the cold side,

looking in, nonplussed, at us,
one pace across the multiverse.

Amused by this night ritual,
we will miss it when you cotton on,

though I still see my double there,
unguarded, open,

coatless in a downpour,
but impervious to weather,

trying to catch my eye.
I never think to let him in.

ELLIPTICS
i.m. I.R.

1

Full-tilt towards infinity, eleven hounds
track the earth's sharp curvature.
No bobtail pelt of hare,
no halt of wounded deer,
not in pursuit, just muzzle down and go
as the world turns towards them.
Dusk that never blossoms.
Endless vespers.

2

Night-long drive.
The road one step ahead.
Picture flowers by your bed:
deca-petalled heartleaf arnica,
child's drawing of a sun, full butter, sweetcorn,
wake up to a morning curtains cannot hold,
world out there for which
we have no words.

3

Houses dark and steep, oblivious –
their street numbers and names
half-lit on gates *three, five, seven, nine* –
now run out into fields.
Love alone brooks resurrection,
nothing else withstands its blaze,
a lock that picks itself.

4

Under our feet, below the sewers,
held by ligaments of a nameless stream,
a doctor-fish heals itself.
Scarred tench stutters into heartbeats,
ons and offs, ones and zeros, hum.
After winter's stasis,
this is life as bulb on the blink,
burnt-out filament,
arcing from silt to float downstream.
Now you become a shoal of *four, six, eight*,
and how salt, how singular,
how like the sea you are.

5

Seven swans in grief alight
on seven highways,
mistaking them for rivers,
cars schooling and shoaling,
pedestrians as trees weep on the banks,
blue lights scale the undersides of bridges.

6

Wildfires on the bare hills.
Three blackbird pairs on startle in their gardens.

7

Like a bird that has hit glass.
Like a rinsed-through,
freeze-dried version of yourself.
Like a loose suit of you

that nobody checked if you wanted to wear.
The wire-wool of your hair.
Pipe-cleaner fingers in a glove of skin.
Not knowing what realm you're in.

8

Be quiet, you say.
Beyond these walls is so much silence.
Damned if I can hear it.

9

On the way,
I reckoned up trios of streetlamps
so as not to be outfaced by multiples.
Every time I thought of you
I lost my thread
and had to start again.

10

Rooks wake, warn and clatter.
Bees like loose wires under roof tiles.
The long-gone and the not-yet-here have better
things to do than pay attention to this room
but if they did they would

11

know this as the punctum
where love can be undone or done,
can be undone or done.

A WINTER INVENTORY

One light left on in the smallest of hours.
A figure behind frosted glass,
reckoning up the comings and goings.

The dark outside is growing crystals.
Longer you look, more you see:

a stunted cactus on the windowsill,
metronome of gutter drips,
broken sycamore embossed on sky.

Beyond the garden, over our fence,
the local school, abandoned, has run wild:

playground seized by moss,
climbing frame by brambles now in fruit,
sports field turned savanna,

goalposts upturned by the grasses,
crossbars like frames of sunken ships.

Thistles burst through tarmac,
nettles up the climbing wall,
desire paths cut by badgers, looters, cats.

More of us were born than ever died.
We still keep our noses ahead of them.

RED SMOKY HEARTS

Having been in hibernation for so long,
for millennia of winters,
– though it felt like an instant,
too quick for atomic clocks –
a wakening starts, no rush, these hearts
have all the time they need.
The ones kept under stone slabs push them up,
wrinkled ones like prunes in jars stir,
those dried to husks in urns,
or atrophied to damsons
pulse and jitter.
Close by, out of sight for now,
drapes are torn from windows,
locks picked, tables laid, doors thrown open.
It all counts, nothing is forgotten.

SOLILOQUY OF A FOCUS-PULLER

Stone with a stone pushed into it,
then a single clay bead, then a string,
an hour-glass, broken barometer
stuck on very dry and still,
dome loupe to get up close,
pinned-up postcard of a man of sorrows

(green-skinned, distended belly,
hands nailed to his breast,
pianist's hands like capsized crabs,
rib-ladder up towards the face,
nestled to its shoulder blade,
a shoulder to cry on, scapula, scalpel,
brow pulled to a skein above
the wishbone of his nose,
eyes dark and pitted as bad fruit
and nothing to show for it
caught in the act of trying to cry)

but it is all too much, a motion blur,
cacophony, if only we could see,
not far but wider, out of frame,
a river after dark, row of black poplars
then domes and towers of a city,
all the people in their finery,
the water is alive, the jewels in it,
then wider, further, out and out.

NOTES & ACKNOWLEDGEMENTS

The epigraphs are taken from the following sources: Iris Murdoch - *The Sea, The Sea*; Walt Whitman - *Song of Myself*; Emily Dickinson - poem 318; Simone Weil - *Gravity and Grace* translated by Arthur Wills.

The reference to 'the loud wild' at the end of **Sumac** is a nod to D.H. Lawrence in *Lady Chatterley's Lover*, when Mellors wakes in the woods: 'He listened to the loud wild calling of blackbirds and thrushes in the wood. It would be a brilliant morning, about half past five, his hour for rising. He had slept so fast! It was such a new day.' The phrase 'red smoky heart' comes from Lawrence's poem 'Eagle in New Mexico', adapted for the title **Red Smoky Hearts**, and **Snow-Remembering Heart** is a phrase from 'Almond Blossom' in his collection *Birds, Beasts and Flowers*.

The mysterious word **Salitter**, with linguistic roots in the explosive compound 'saltpetre', appears in the work of Jakob Böhme as a divine substance through which God creates matter from absence. It can be used, as in Cormac McCarthy's *The Road*, to refer to the essence of God.

'Agouti' in **Two Women Walk a Himalayan Wolf** is a speckled or grizzled kind of animal fur made up light and dark bands.

Mandelstam Variables is a term from theoretical physics. It refers to a method of coding the energy of particles in scattering processes, developed by physicist Stanley Mandelstam. I took the name 'Mandelstam variables', and the notion of a scattering process, as a good account of this sequence of *very* free versions of – and riffs off – some of Osip Mandelstam's poems with his characteristic cast of birds, beasts and flowers. To my knowledge Stanley was no relation of Osip.

I became aware of the phrase **Metaphysical Animals**, and the ideas behind it, through Clare Mac Cumhaill and Rachael Wiseman's book – *Metaphysical Animals: How Four Women Brought Philosophy Back to Life* – on the impact of philosophers Elizabeth Anscombe, Mary Midgley, Philippa Foot and Iris Murdoch.

The German word 'eigengrau' in **Greys** refers to 'intrinsic grey' a background colour seen in absolute darkness, so even in the absence of light the brain sees colour.

The title **Kiss on Wood** is a variation on the liturgical term for veneration of the cross in Good Friday rituals. It is also a nod to James MacMillan's meditation for violin and piano 'Kiss on Wood'.

The doctor, Astrov, referred to in **Astrov's Maps** is a character in Chekhov's *Uncle Vanya*.

On the night of 25 May 1940, scientists at Oxford University's Dunn School of Pathology conducted an experiment on **Eight Lab Mice**, all injected with streptococcus bacteria, in which four were treated with penicillin and four left untreated. This led to the breakthrough development of penicillin to fight infections in humans and animals. Mus Musculus is the most common breed of laboratory mice. The italicised sections in this poem are based on the lab journals of scientist Norman Heatley from that night.

In **Free Dive**, the word 'byss', as the opposite of 'abyss', but also as a way of describing the seafloor, is a reference to the word 'ungrund' in 17th-century mystic Jakob Böhme's work, which refers to a groundless, formless void before the existence of anything – including God – an emptiness from which all matter, being and reality emerges.

Elliptics is in memory of my mother Iris.

★

I'm very grateful to the editors of publications in which these poems, some in earlier versions, appeared: *Bad Lilies*, BBC Radio 4, *Poetry London*, *PN Review*, the *Tablet*, *Times Literary Supplement*. 'Elliptics' was set to music by the composer Emily Howard and nominated for an Ivor Novello Award. Some of these poems arose from a collaboration with the photographer Norman McBeath. Others were informed by conversations with scientists at the Dunn School of Pathology at Oxford University, as part of a text and music project commissioned by Lincoln College, Oxford. 'Aquarium' first appeared in *Imagination in an Age of Crisis*, edited by Jason Goroncy and Rod Pattenden.